# Stoic Team Building

## Fostering Collaboration, Trust, and Resilience

# Table of Contents

# Chapter 1. Introduction

Step into the empowering world of Stoicism and discover how it can transform your team dynamics in ways you've never imagined. This Special Report on "Stoic Team Building: Fostering Collaboration, Trust, and Resilience," captures the essence of applying ancient Stoic wisdom to modern team building, ultimately leading to more integrated, reliable, and robust teams. Through tales of enduring Stoic principle, insights from successful implementation, and a comprehensive guide on practicing stoicism within your professional sphere, this report is a must-have for leaders aspiring to create steadfast and resilient teams. So, buckle up and get ready to traverse the path less travelled, and you will likely find it making all the difference. 'Buy' this report today and unleash a level of collaboration, trust, encouragement and resilience your team has yet to experience!

# Chapter 2. The Fundamentals of Stoicism

The ancient philosophy of Stoicism has a surprising amount to offer in the modern world, particularly within the context of building strong, collaborative teams. Stoicism teaches us to focus on what's within our control, to remain unperturbed by external events, and to cultivate virtues such as wisdom, courage, justice, and temperance. These principles, when appropriately applied to a team environment, can foster cohesion, trust, and resilience.

## 2.1. The Four Virtues of Stoicism

The foundation of Stoicism rests on four key virtues—wisdom, courage, justice, and temperance—that help to shape its philosophical underpinning and can significantly influence today's team dynamics.

1. **Wisdom**: This is the understanding of the nature of things—what is good, what is evil, and what is neither. In a team environment, wisdom means understanding the skills, strengths, and limitations of team members, operational guidelines, market scenarios, client demands, etc., to make informed decisions and create workable strategies.

2. **Courage**: This refers not only to physical courage but also to moral courage - sticking to ethical principles and standing against wrongdoing. In professional life, courage reflects taking on challenging tasks, standing up for the team, and making tough decisions for the overall benefit.

3. **Justice**: It consists of treating everyone impartially and giving them their due. Justice in team dynamics means maintaining a fair process, ensuring equal opportunities to all members, and addressing any cases of favoritism or discrimination.

4. **Temperance**: It is the ability to exercise due measure in all things—avoiding extremes of behavior or emotion. Within a team, temperance can relate to managing emotions at work, balancing work and rest, or avoiding the extreme positions in discussions and negotiations.

These virtues are guidelines for how we should conduct ourselves, and Stoicism argues that practicing these virtues leads to eudaimonia—that is, a good and flourishing life.

## 2.2. Dichotomy of Control

The dichotomy of control is a fundamental principle of Stoicism, which differentiates between what is in our control and what is not. Things in our control are related to our minds—our beliefs, judgments, desires, and the actions we choose to take or avoid. Things not in our control include external events—the actions of others, reputation, weather, past events, etc.

In a team context, understanding this dichotomy can help in releasing anxiety over uncontrollable events, focusing energy on manageable aspects, and maintaining tranquility when faced with challenging circumstances. For instance, a project manager may not be able to control a client's requirements (external), but they can certainly control their team's response to those requirements (internal).

## 2.3. Dealing with Emotions in Stoicism

Stoicism teaches us that our emotions are not driven by events themselves, but by our judgments of those events. This shift in perspective suggests that by changing our judgments, we can change our responses.

Teams can adopt this by promoting a mindset where members perceive challenges as opportunities to learn and grow, rather than as roadblocks. By doing this, team members can manage their reactions better, leading to less stress and more productivity.

# 2.4. Stoic Practices

In order to cultivate stoic principles within a team, practical exercises are essential. Some effective practices include:

- **Preparation**: Anticipating potential difficulties helps teams deal with them effectively when they arise.

- **Self-reflection**: Reflecting on one's thoughts and actions aids self-improvement and encourages mutual understanding within the team.

- **Objective Representation**: Seeing things as they are, without adding exaggerated positive or negative interpretations, promotes realistic expectations and plans.

- **Stoic Meditation**: Examining one's judgments and analyzing their validity encourages clearer thinking and lessens unhelpful reactions to events.

By understanding and implementing these fundamental principles and practices of Stoicism, teams can foster a collaborative environment built on mutual respect, shared understanding, and unconditional perseverance. Above all, they can cultivate the kind of resilience and adaptability necessary to thrive in the face of ever-changing corporate landscapes.

# Chapter 3. Stoicism and Team Building: The Untold Connection

Stoicism, an ancient philosophy, has offered generations of individuals a way of looking at the world that fosters resilience, calmness, and indeed a level of detachment beneficial to navigating the ebbs and flows of life. Perhaps less well known is how these powerful principles can be applied to team dynamics, creating a sense of equilibrium, collaboration and productivity within the professional realm. This report will delve into this compelling intertwine, dissecting how stoicism can shape, nurture and reinforce an efficient and powerful team.

## 3.1. The Roots of Stoicism

Stoicism, as a philosophy, dates back to ancient Greece and Rome. It emphasizes the vital importance of self-control, virtue, and adapting to what you cannot control. The stoics taught that our reactions, rather than circumstances themselves, cause most of our troubles. They upheld the belief that life's adversities can stimulate personal growth if we respond to challenges with wisdom, integrity, and serenity.

To delve deeper, three primary pillars uphold Stoic philosophy:

1. Rationality: The belief in making decisions grounded in logic rather than emotion, ensuring actions lean towards virtue and wisdom.

2. Acceptance: Recognizing the dichotomy of control – the ability to differentiate between situations within our control and those beyond it. The former should ignite action and the latter

dispassion.

3. Virtue: The objective of virtuous actions, actions brimming not from self-serving tendencies but from a place of kindness, integrity, courage and wisdom - the four cardinal virtues of stoicism.

# 3.2. Stoicism in the Workplace: Why it Matters

In the fast-paced modern workplace, the principles of Stoicism offer an oasis of calm and rationale. Fostering rationality, stoicism allows teams to prioritize tasks better, while acceptance creates a more tranquil workplace — one where hurdles are met with composed solutions rather than reactive responses. The pursuit of virtue helps to align team members with the broader organizational goals, developing a purpose-driven work atmosphere that values contributions to the group over individual achievements.

# 3.3. Stoic Team Dynamics: Creating a Resilient Workplace

How, you might wonder, can an ancient philosophy impact something as modern and dynamic as team-building?

By encouraging emotional intelligence, fostering resilience, preventing burnout, and facilitating more effective communication, Stoicism's principles prove invaluable when integrated into a team's ethos.

1. Emotional intelligence: Stoicism trains individuals to respond rather than react, prioritizing rationality over emotional whims. This emotional intelligence aids in understanding and addressing the emotions of team members, reducing misunderstandings and

effectively facilitating communication.

2. Resilience: The Stoic tenet of recognizing the dichotomy of control helps build resilience in teams. It enables teams to pivot during challenging situations, acknowledging areas outside their influence and focusing energy on what they can change.

3. Preventing burnout: Stoic philosophy encourages acceptance of circumstances beyond our control, thereby lowering stress arising from unrealistic expectations. This acceptance can significantly reduce team burnout, fostering a harmonious and balanced workplace environment.

4. Effective Communication: Stoicism's emphasis on listening over speaking nurtures more balanced and inclusive communication. It champions understanding over being understood, minimizing conflicts and nurturing solid relationships.

# 3.4. Stoicism in Action: A Step-by-Step Guide

Integrating Stoicism into team building is a process. Here's a step-by-step guide to get you started:

1. Introduction to Stoicism: Conduct workshops or learning sessions about Stoic philosophy. Aim to familiarize your team with the principles of Stoicism and its potential benefits.

2. Implementation of Stoic Principles: Begin to incorporate Stoic principles into daily tasks and general work behavior. This can vary from encouraging mindful responses to building a culture of virtue-driven actions.

3. Constant Reinforcement: Consistent reinforcement is key for the successful inculcation of Stoic principles. Regular discussions or quick catch-up sessions to evaluate the progress of Stoic practice within the team can be valuable.

4. Feedback and Adaptation: Establish a two-way channel for your team to share their experiences, thoughts, and insights around this new practice. Use this feedback to adapt and tailor the Stoic principles to the team's unique dynamics.

In conclusion, Stoicism, with its powerful tenets, offers a resilient, balanced, and more harmonious framework for team dynamics. As we journey into embracing Stoicism in the workplace, we uncover a more serene, logical, and virtue-driven team poised to face any challenges with grace and composure itself. We must remember, in the end, that the best way for teams to adopt Stoicism is by embodying its principles in our own leadership – because the best leadership, after all, is one that leads by example.

# Chapter 4. Cultivating Resilience through Stoic Teachings

The notion of resilience goes hand in hand with the philosophy of Stoicism. Sage Stoics gifted the world with invaluable wisdom on how to build untapped resilience, shaping an almost indomitable spirit that would prove instrumental in enabling us to confront the myriad of challenges life and work can throw our way. We'll explore these teachings and how they can be incorporated into team building to create more robust entities ready to face any challenge.

## 4.1. Empathy & Understanding: The Power Tools of Stoicism

The mainstay of Stoicism is empathy and understanding, powerful tools often underestimated in the team-building landscape. Stoic teachings assert the importance of seeing things from different perspectives, understanding that each individual is fighting their own internal battles, and drawing strength from empathetic interactions. These principles can be applied in team settings to foster more empathetic exchanges, thus creating a more supportive and understanding work environment.

In simple terms, empathy could be the most potent tool in overcoming interpersonal hurdles in a team. By acknowledging individual struggles, we strive to create an environment in which team members perceive challenges not as personal attacks, but as shared obstacles that can be optimistically managed. Thus, fostering resilience against professional or personal difficulties through the assimilation of empathetic understanding at the team level.

## 4.2. The Dichotomy of Control: Focusing on What Matters

An essential tenet of Stoic philosophy is the 'dichotomy of control,' identifying what one can and cannot control. It's about shifting focus from the uncontrollable to the controllable aspects of work and life.

When translated into a team setting, the dichotomy of control could serve as a guide for delineating roles and responsibilities. By helping individuals identify aspects within their control, teams can concentrate on their actions and improve their efficiency. This focus on what can be controlled, combined with the acceptance of what can't, cultivates resilience and reduces unnecessary stress and conflict within the team.

To integrate this teaching within a team manifesto, leaders may conduct "control mapping" sessions, where each team member examines their direct sphere of control. These sessions aid in creating transparent communication channels, fostering trust among members and thus bolstering collective resilience.

## 4.3. Facing Adversity: The Stoic Perspective

Stoics saw adversity not as misfortune but as an opportunity for growth. Translating this perspective into team dynamics creates space for failure, encouraging risk-taking while also building resilience to confront setbacks.

To cultivate this environment, a start could be regular team discussions where failures are shared, dissected, and learned from, rather than being swept under the rug. Referred to as 'failure forums,' these create a secure space for vulnerability, adaptation, and subsequently, resilience. By reframing the discourse around failure within teams, we trade fear and defensiveness for collective learning and growth, making room for unmatched resilience.

# 4.4. Emotion Regulation: The Stoic Stance

Stoics held a profound understanding of emotions and their regulation, a concept of great relevance to team dynamics. They practiced "prosochē" or "mindfulness" to anticipate emotional responses and exercise control. By managing our reactions, we can mitigate harm to team relationships and maintain a supportive and productive work atmosphere.

To ingrain this principle into team culture, concepts like 'emotion wheel' workshops could be useful. The core idea of such exercises is to help members identify and articulate their emotional states better. The process not only provides an understanding of personal emotions but also opens empathetic conversations within the team, leading to better conflict management and overall emotional resilience.

# 4.5. The Role of Virtue in Team Interactions

Virtue, according to Stoics, is the highest form of goodness and our ultimate purpose. It guides behavior and attitudes, while also dictating how we interact with others, making it crucial in team environments. To integrate virtue within a team, leaders can encourage adherence to a set of shared values reflective of Stoic virtues - wisdom, courage, justice, and temperance.

This adherence to virtue encourages members to act with integrity and work towards the collective goal, rather than individual gain. Endorsing virtue in team interactions and methodologies promotes altruistic behavior, strengthens bonds, and contributes significantly to resilience.

In essence, the value Stoic philosophy brings to team dynamics is insurmountable. From fostering empathy and understanding to imparting the lesson of control, promoting a growth mentality in the face of adversity, and endorsing virtue-driven interactions, Stoic teachings forge teams defined by trust, collaboration, and, most importantly, resilience. By nurturing these teachings, we inch towards creating workspaces that value human connection, celebrate diversity, and uphold resilience as a surviving strategy, leading to incredible productivity and happiness.

# Chapter 5. The Art of Collaboration: Stoic Techniques

Stoic philosophy, despite being ancient, holds techniques and insights that are remarkably relevant to today's dynamic and challenging team environments. At the heart of Stoicism lie principles and ideas that can bolster the collaborative efforts of any team, forging understanding, unity, and resilience. Certainly, a deep dive into these techniques is in order.

## 5.1. Embracing Amor Fati: Love of Fate

Amor Fati, the Love of Fate, is the first stoic concept we consider. It encourages us to accept and love everything that happens, viewing our fate not as a burden but as an opportunity for growth and development. In a team setting, this attitude can help eliminate unnecessary conflict and foster a powerful, unified approach to tackling challenges.

Consider disagreements that often rise during brainstorming sessions or project planning meetings. Problems occur when team members view these disagreements as obstacles rather than opportunities to learn. By embracing Amor Fati, teams can learn to appreciate these differing viewpoints, thus leading to innovative solutions drawn from diverse perspectives.

# 5.2. The Dichotomy of Control: Knowing What We Can Change

Stoicism teaches us the importance of understanding and accepting what we can and cannot influence. This is called the Dichotomy of Control. It's a simple yet profound rule: focus your energy and efforts on what can be changed, and accept what cannot.

In the context of a team, this understanding removes significant contributors to internal strife. The focus shifts from blame and frustration to construction and collaboration. The collective energy of the team hones in on strategies and solutions, leading to a cohesive, effective group that is not derailed by circumstances beyond their control.

# 5.3. Practicing Sympatheia: Unity in Action

Sympatheia is a concept that describes the interdependence of all things in the world. It's the recognition that we're all part of a bigger ecosystem, each playing our part to contribute to a greater whole. When applied to a team, Sympatheia fosters a sense of unity, collaboration, and mutual support.

To achieve this, leaders should help their team understand how each member's role contributes to the bigger picture. When team members see how their work is interconnected and how they depend on each other's efforts, it increases their willingness to collaborate and support each other.

## 5.4. Using Premeditatio Malorum to Build Resilience

Premeditatio Malorum is a technique where one visualizes the worst that could happen in any given situation. It helps to build resilience, not through pessimism, but through preparedness and realism.

Teams can apply this technique in their planning and preparation stages. By anticipating possible challenges or obstacles, teams can devise effective strategies to overcome them. This allows the team to be better prepared and more resilient in the face of adversity, enhancing their ability to work together towards their goal.

## 5.5. Learning from the Principle of Summum Bonum

Summum Bonum, or the highest good, is a fundamental concept in Stoicism. It signifies that virtue and character are the highest values to aspire to. In a team, this means that a person's character and actions, their contribution to the team dynamic, and their commitment to delivering quality work, should be valued above all else.

This principle builds a culture of trust and respect, wherein team members feel valued for who they are and what they bring to the table. It fosters an environment where collaboration thrives, and people feel connected to the collective purpose.

In conclusion, each of these Stoic principles serves as a versatile, practical, and effective tool for enhancing collaboration within teams. By embodying and promoting Amor Fati, the Dichotomy of Control, Sympatheia, Premeditatio Malorum, and Summum Bonum, teams can deeply enhance their collaborative capacity. These methods keep the teams in harmony, focused on the task at hand,

and resilient in dealing with challenges - an unbeatable combination for driving team success and longevity.

# Chapter 6. Shaping Trust: Stoic Perspectives

Trust is the lifeblood of effective teamwork. Building trust, however, can often be challenging. For that, the stoic philosophy can provide valuable insights and actionable techniques towards fostering lasting trust in team environments.

## 6.1. Trust and the Stoic Dichotomy of Control

Stoicism teaches about the 'dichotomy of control', a principle that differentiates between what one can and cannot control. In the context of trust-building, it implies that while you cannot control others' actions, you can control your responses, integrity, and honesty, all necessary for establishing trust.

The dichotomy of control also focuses on letting go of unproductive worries about matters out of our hands. In team settings, practicing this principle can lead to trusting others' capabilities and fostering a non-toxic, blame-free environment.

Being aware of this principle helps team members become more accepting of others, acknowledging their strengths and weaknesses without prejudgment. This openness nurtures mutual trust, promoting an inclusive team environment, and boosting collaboration and productivity.

## 6.2. The Role of Virtues in Building Trust

The Stoics propose four fundamental virtues: wisdom, courage, justice, and temperance. The application of these virtues can enhance trust within a team.

- Wisdom: Using logic, discernment, and understanding in interpersonal interactions to solve team disputes and work towards shared goals.

- Courage: Demonstrating reliability by facing challenges and showing commitment to team objectives.

- Justice: Treating all team members fairly and impartially, fostering an atmosphere of mutual respect.

- Temperance: Exercising self-control and moderation to avoid disproportionate reactions or toxic behaviors.

Trust can be significantly augmented when these virtues are implemented in team dynamics.

# 6.3. Stoicism and Trust in Leadership

In firms where leaders critically identify their values and consistently act in step with these principles, employees develop more trust in the leadership. Here are some facets of stoic leadership supporting trust-building:

- Transparent communication: Leaders who communicate honestly, openly, and regularly with their team members foster trust.

- Being consistent: Leaders following a stoic philosophy maintain their composure under pressure, bolstering team confidence in their leadership.

- Leading by example: Leaders embodying stoic virtues of wisdom, justice, courage, and temperance inspire trust and respect among team members.

Leaders who practice stoicism also respect and consider their team members' opinions, further solidifying mutual trust.

# 6.4. Embracing Adversity: The Path to Resilience and Trust

Stoicism encourages us to perceive adversity as an opportunity for learning and growth. Challenging situations reveal hidden strengths and encourage teams to come together, fostering reciprocal trust.

A team leader practicing stoicism maintains a composed and confident demeanor in the face of adversity, reinforcing the team's trust in their leadership. Also, by encouraging team members to view adversity through a stoic lens, leaders can cultivate resilience and deepen trust within the team.

# 6.5. Stoicism and Trust: Addressing Misunderstandings

Misunderstandings can negatively impact trust. However, stoicism offers a tool to address this - the idea of 'seeing things as they are.'

A stoic practices objective observation and tries to understand situations without bias or preconceived notions. Implementing this perspective within a team can lead to more constructive conversations, improved conflict resolution, and ultimately, stronger trust among team members.

In conclusion, stoic teachings proffer a wealth of strategies and insights that can help build and foster trust within teams. By internalizing and acting upon these principles, leaders can create a culture of trust, openness, and mutual respect, and create robust, high-performing teams.

# Chapter 7. Case Studies: Successful Stoic Team Building Implementations

The use and application of Stoic principles in team building have led to remarkable results within numerous organizations. Detailed below are several case studies that highlight how Stoic concepts have been used effectively to foster collaboration, trust, and resilience amongst team members.

## 7.1. Case Study 1: TechX - Building Trust Through Stoic Principles

TechX, a leading technology startup, was struggling with team dynamics. Despite having a batch of highly talented individuals, the organization found difficult to maintain trust and transparency within the teams.

To overcome these obstacles, TechX's management decided to employ Stoic principles in their team building efforts. They focussed on three key concepts - understanding what is in one's control, practicing objectivity and acceptance, and demonstrating courage.

The organization encouraged team members to focus on actions within their control and letting go of fears of failure that were largely external. By promoting objective reasoning and acceptance, they encouraged open communication and transparency. The emphasis on courage further made employees feel validated, pushing them to freely share their ideas and criticisms.

The results of this implementation were striking. Almost immediately, there was a great improvement in team cohesion and transparency. Over time, this led to a higher level of trust among team members, thereby increasing overall productivity and innovation within the organization.

## 7.2. Case Study 2: InnoMax - Driving Collaboration Using Stoicism

InnoMax, a leading product innovation company, struggled with silos and lack of collaboration within its teams. Inter-departmental communication was lacking, causing constant misunderstanding and conflicts.

To tackle this, InnoMax brought Stoic principles to the front line, focusing on wisdom, acceptance, and empathy. They adopted an approach where team members were expected to comprehend the strengths and weaknesses of each other, thereby using this knowledge to leverage collaboration.

Practices such as group discussions centered on understanding and accepting the diverse skills and perspectives of each member were frequently organized. Moreover, through constant demonstrative empathy exercises, employees were urged to step into each other's shoes.

InnoMax began witnessing a more supportive work environment where employees willingly offered assistance to each other, thereby breaking the silos previously formed. The increased collaboration eventually led to a noticeable improvement in innovation and swift execution of ideas, significantly raising the company's growth rate.

## 7.3. Case Study 3: HealthPlus - Fostering Resilience in Tough Times

HealthPlus, a global healthcare corporation, faced major setbacks when the global pandemic struck. The move to remote working, coupled with the general fear and uncertainty, weighed heavy on the teams.

In response to this crisis, HealthPlus utilized stoicism to foster resilience amongst their teams. They concentrated on three Stoic tenets - viewing adversity as an opportunity to grow, learning to let go of what's not within their control, and fostering equanimity to maintain calm in times of difficulty.

Virtual seminars and workshops on stoic philosophies were held to help employees build resilience. Copious resources were circulated that emphasized seeing difficulties as opportunities to learn and grow. Employees were encouraged to differentiate between what's within and outside their control, thereby reducing unnecessary stress.

Through these efforts, HealthPlus noticed an uptick in overall team resilience and morale. Despite the crisis, employees bounced back, and productivity was maintained as teams learned to accept and navigate the new normal with a Stoic mindset.

In conclusion, the application of Stoic principles can significantly enhance team dynamics, as evidenced by these case studies. By developing understanding, trust, and resilience, teams can transform into truly integrated, reliable, and robust units.

# Chapter 8. From Theory to Practice: Incorporating Stoicism in Daily Activities

In the thrilling journey of Stoic inspiration and application, one needs to step beyond just knowing the concepts, to integrating them into the very fabric of everyday activities. This practical engagement with Stoic principles converts theoretical understanding into tangible experiences, forever altering our perception and response to the world around us, and more specifically, our team dynamics.

## 8.1. Embracing the Dichotomy of Control

Incorporating Stoicism into daily activities begins with a fundamental principle: the Dichotomy of Control. Coined by ancient Stoic philosopher Epictetus, it argues that events are divided into what we can control—in essence, our thoughts, feelings and actions—and what we cannot control, namely, everything else. A key step to embracing this philosophy is regular self-evaluation.

Keep a personal journal to document your thoughts, feelings, and experiences. This not just enhances self-awareness but also helps distinguish between controllable and uncontrollable factors. Following this, focus your energies on aspects within your control. This shift in perspective remarkably reduces stress levels and enhances personal satisfaction, thereby reflecting positively on your interactions within the team.

## 8.2. Cultivating Virtuous Actions

Characterizing virtuous actions as the highest good, the Stoics emphasize cultivating virtues of wisdom, courage, justice, and temperance. These virtues hold immense importance in the professional world in fostering trust and collaborative work environments.

Consider setting personal daily targets based on these virtues to embed them into your professional life. For instance, work towards making one 'just' decision a day or showcasing 'courage' by voicing your ideas in team meetings. Make sure to jot down these endeavors in your personal journal, reflecting on their accomplishment.

Additionally, team leads can structure exercises and discussions inspired by these virtues into daily stand-up meetings. This conscious effort to showcase and acknowledge stoic virtues will invoke a supportive atmosphere conducive to overall team growth.

## 8.3. Implementing the Negative Visualization Technique

Negative visualization isn't about pessimism. In contrast, it aids in appreciating the present and mitigating the impact of potential negative events.

In the context of project management, it could be about visualizing potential pitfalls and strategizing how to face and overcome them. During brainstorming sessions, encourage your team to envisage possible challenges and craft contingency plans. The negative visualization technique equips teams with the proactive capacity to manage setbacks or changes, enhancing resilience.

# 8.4. Neutralizing the Perception of External Events

Our impressions of external events can significantly impact our reaction. As a Stoic, we should train ourselves to see situations objectively, eliminating emotional bias. Metaphorically, events are like a piece of wax, taking the shape of whatever belief presses against them.

As a team member or leader, when unexpected events occur, pause, evaluate, and respond instead of outright reacting. This will help you take informed decisions that are best for your team and the project rather than getting swayed by initial emotions.

To cultivate this quality in your team, integrate short mindfulness activities in the workplace. You could schedule a 5 minute breather before team meetings where everyone silently observes their thoughts, or introduce a quick 'Meditation Minute' during breaks.

# 8.5. Accepting Fate with Serenity

The Stoic's tranquillity rests in accepting things as they are, surrendering to the natural order—the Fate. In corporate terms, this could mean embracing company policies, market trends, or even teammates' temperaments. Encouraging an acceptance mindset within your team could mean fewer skirmishes, enhanced cooperation, and better flexibility in changing circumstances.

Incorporate exercises where team members list factors they cannot control yet profoundly impact their work. Follow it with a discussion to help team members understand each other's challenges and narratives, building empathy and a better team spirit.

The everyday application of Stoicism is not just about individual change but also affecting the larger team culture, creating a safe, resilient, and harmonious work atmosphere. Following the Stoic way ensures that teams can deliver their best under any circumstances, highlighting the valiant principles these ancient Greek philosophers had shared with the world. This practical embodiment of Stoic principles melds with the professional landscape, making it more resilient, mindful, adaptable, and above all, stoically successful. Remember, change starts with you, and the effort to transform your team's dynamic should begin at a personal level.

# Chapter 9. Stoic Problem-Solving: Bridging Discord and Encouraging Unity

Ever since its birth in ancient Greece, Stoicism has been cherished for teaching the art of inner resilience and the value of clear, objective thinking - vital skills when it comes to problem-solving. It is within the power of every team to adapt these millennia-old insights to contemporary challenges. The training ground of Stoicism is the world itself, making every issue an opportunity to learn, grow, and apply Stoic wisdom.

## 9.1. Stoicism - A Catalyst for Effective Problem-Solving

Stoicism is not merely a theoretical philosophy; rather, it's a pragmatic, real-world philosophy that encourages us to rise above the chaos and confusion, fostering clarity and judgement. These qualities are paramount to effective problem-solving. A Stoic's approach involves cultivating an objective understanding, practical wisdom, self-control, and a moral purpose, all beautifully synthesized in the daily experiences of a team.

To enhance problem-solving capabilities, it's crucial to embrace the Stoic principle of amathia. In ancient Greek, amathia means 'ignorance of what is right', and the Stoics believed that wrong actions are the result of such ignorance. A great team always shows a desire to learn, reflect, and transform to eradicate this ignorance, leveraging shared knowledge and wisdom. In Stoic terms, this means focusing on continuous improvement, which is the cornerstone of effective problem-solving.

## 9.2. The Dichotomy of Control in Problem-Solving

Epictetus, a key proponent of Stoicism, formulated the 'dichotomy of control' dictum, which says, "Some things are up to us, and some things are not". This simple but profound perception is pivotal in problem-solving. Teams often spend endless hours worrying and procrastinating on things beyond their control, thus losing sight of what's most important – solving the issue at hand.

By acknowledging and accepting what we can't control, teams can focus on what they can: their responses, steps to resolution, and learning outcomes. This shift in focus eradicates conflicts and disagreements in the team, fostering unity and a problem-solving mindset.

## 9.3. Stoic Virtues and Collaborative Problem-Solving

Applying Stoic virtues to problem-solving offers an exemplar of collaborative functioning. Let's see how:

1. Wisdom: In Stoicism, wisdom is the knowledge of what is good, what is bad, and what is neutral. A wise team separates facts from opinions, focuses on the context, and avoids being swayed by prejudice. Wisdom also encompasses open-mindedness, making teams adaptable and ready for change.

2. Courage: The courage to question, challenge, and innovate is pivotal in problem-solving. Courage doesn't eliminate fear of failure or disagreements but channels it constructively to work through difficulties.

3. Justice: Fairness and equality breed trust among team members. Transparency, empathy, and active listening promote a sense of

shared responsibility and light the path to conflict resolution.

4. Temperance: Temperance moderates extreme reactions, helping teams maintain equilibrium even amidst adversities. It promotes patience, understanding, and restraint, integral qualities for smooth and efficient problem-solving.

# 9.4. Encouraging Unity through Stoic Meditations

Finally, an integral part of Stoicism, its meditations, can provide a systematic way to handle discord and promote unity amongst teams. Meditations such as the View from Above, Premeditation of Adversities, and the Practice of Negative Visualization not only instill a sense of calmness and contemplation but also inculcate a habit of viewing problems from myriad perspectives - a key skill in any problem-solving process.

As our exploration of 'Stoic Problem-Solving: Bridging Discord and Encouraging Unity' comes to an end, it's clear that embracing Stoic principles can transform how teams face challenges. Stoicism, with its focus on rational thought, control, virtues, and meditation, provides an all-encompassing roadmap to effective problem-solving. By implementing these principles, teams can not only conquer any obstacle that comes their way but also foster an environment of trust, resilience, and unity.

# Chapter 10. Selene-Tested Methods: Stoic Strategies for Team Motivation

In the wake of appreciating the tenets of stoicism, it becomes indispensable to enlist stoic strategies tested by high-performing teams and leaders, over the centuries. These timeless techniques prove instrumental in fostering motivation, collaboration, and resilience among team members.

## 10.1. The Dichotomy of Control

A concept that succinctly encapsulates the Stoic outlook towards life is the Dichotomy of Control - the understanding that some events lie in one's control while others don't. Identifying and accepting this in team environments is crucial for team motivation. Instead of focusing on things outside of their control such as market fluctuations, client opinions, or competitor actions, teams must concentrate on their capabilities; consistently improving their skills, refining strategies, and enhancing inter-team communications. This shift in focus enables teams to foster resilience and channel their energy productivamente, consequently amplifying team motivation.

## 10.2. The View from Above

This Stoic technique involves visualizing challenging situations from a broader perspective. Typically, stepping back to observe an organizational hiccup enables the team to maintain calm and avoid knee-jerk reactions. By reinforcing the transient nature of the issue, leaders can motivate their teams to devise innovative solutions rather than get disheartened. The view from above also helps align the team's objectives with the organization's goals, promoting unity and shared ownership of successes and failures.

## 10.3. Premeditation of Evils (Premeditatio Malorum)

By expecting potential setbacks, teams can prepare adequately for their mitigation and avoid being caught off guard. Foreseeing potential hindrances enables a proactive approach, fostering resilience, and guarding against demotivation during challenging times. Moreover, this practice of envisaging worst-case scenarios mitigates the impacts of failure, as the team can strategize on robust backup plans.

## 10.4. Using Nature as a Guide

Emphasizing the natural abilities and talents of each team member rather than their shortcomings allows teams to foster an environment built on trust and respect. A leader acknowledging and leveraging these innate skills and capacities stimulates a sense of confidence within the team. A Stoic team is well versed with each member's unique skill set, which proves invaluable when distributing tasks or during crisis management.

## 10.5. Practicing Discomfort

Promoting the spirit of stepping out of comfort zones can stimulate innovation and growth within teams. When employees are encouraged to take calculated risks and pursue challenging projects, they tend to explore and expand their capabilities. Over time, such teams learn to adapt quickly, enhancing their resilience, thereby bolstering team motivation.

## 10.6. Reflexive Discomfort

When failure or setback strikes, stoic teams are encouraged to reflect and understand the cause and effect. This stoic strategy aims at transforming mistakes into learning opportunities. Subsequently, it transforms the team culture, enabling a shift from perceiving failures as threats, to viewing them as stepping stones towards success and growth.

## 10.7. Vigilant Decision Making

Stoic teams aim to practice thoughtful decision making. The emphasis here is on making collective decisions which are not just informed by data but are also ethically correct. This stoic strategy entails a careful examination of motivations, possible outcomes, and the team's ability to take responsibility for the consequences, ultimately fostering trust and collective effort.

## 10.8. Voluntary Discomfort as a Team

In the corporate world, teams usually strive for comfort, but periodic discomfort can in fact be beneficial. Embarking on challenging projects as a team can foster stronger bonds and crystallize the sense of shared goals. Stoic leaders often use team-bonding activities outside of the comfortable office environment to teach resilience, for example, team hikes or volunteering for a social cause.

## 10.9. Turning Obstacles into Opportunities

Stoicism teaches that everything that happens is an opportunity for growth or a lesson to learn from. Encourage your team to expand their mindset beyond the problem and look for hidden opportunities. This is best done as a group activity where different viewpoints on a challenge are discussed and the team aligns on the most positive interpretation.

By integrating these stoic strategies into team dynamics, leaders can transform their teams into more resilient, motivated, and effective units. While the path may be challenging, the resulting empowerment and resilience are promising rewards. Endeavoring and persevering on this stoic journey paves the way for realizing extraordinary teamwork capabilities.

# Chapter 11. Building the Future: Envisioning Stoic Teams in Modern Workplaces

Stoicism is more than a philosophy; it's a mindset. Advocates of stoicism believe strongly in understanding and controlling their responses instead of changing their circumstances, a principle that can dynamically transform modern workplaces.

The ancient wisdom contained within Stoicism can help shape the future of our work cultures, anchoring teams on resilience, empathy, and synergy. It can make workforces more resilient to change, more attuned to each other's needs, and ultimately, more productive.

## 11.1. Stoicism: A Brief Overview

Originating from ancient Greece, Stoicism is a philosophy predicated on virtues of wisdom, courage, justice, and temperance. Its main focus is teaching one to detach from uncontrolled emotions and desires, seeking peace and tranquility instead. At the root, it's about understanding things we can control and letting go of the things we can't. These principles are pertinent to modern workplaces, translating directly into increased productivity, improved interpersonal relationships, and heightened job satisfaction.

## 11.2. Stoicism in Practice: Bridging Ancient Wisdom and Modern Workplaces

Transcending centuries, the stoic principles are just as relevant today, especially in unraveling team dynamics. As teams are essentially groups of individuals working towards a common goal, it's crucial these individuals can self-regulate, empathize with others, and stay resilient in the face of adversity, all of which are fundamental teachings of Stoicism.

Firstly, Stoicism teaches acceptance, implying that we should not waste time and energy railing against things outside our control. For instance, if a project deadline is moved up, rather than stressing, a stoic team would work on recalibrating their plans.

Secondly, it emphasizes resilience, guiding us to view obstacles as opportunities for learning instead of barriers that hinder progress. This mindset can enable teams to bounce back from failures, interpret them as valuable feedback, and use that to fuel future improvements.

Finally, the stoic concept of 'Sympatheia' - a profound sense of interconnectedness and shared fate - can significantly enhance team collaboration. Embracing this notion would encourage empathy and mutual respect, increasing effectiveness in achieving team goals.

# 11.3. Building Resilience: The Stoic Way

Resilience is imperative within teams. It's the trait that allows us to maintain equanimity and perform even when under stress, making it paramount for maintaining productivity during challenging times. Stoicism enables a shift in perspective towards problems, encouraging us to see them not as impediments, but as opportunities for growth.

To foster resilience, it is essential to establish a culture where failures are not ridiculed but seen as steps towards success. Regular communication within the team regarding potential issues and brainstorming solutions preemptively can help build a more resilient workforce.

## 11.4. Networking with Empathy: The Power of Sympatheia

Integrating Stoicism into modern workplaces also includes embracing the virtue of 'Sympatheia.' Encouraging empathy amongst members can boost connection, leading to enhanced collaboration and overall team success.

It is imperative to create a safe, judgment-free environment for everyone in the team. Regular team-building activities that reinforce mutual understanding and respect can help cultivate a culture of empathy within the team.

## 11.5. Redefining Success: The Stoic Perspective

In line with stoicism, redefine the parameters of success from an outcome-centric model to a virtue-centric one. As team leaders, appreciate and reward not just the result but the virtues displayed throughout the process, such as diligence, honesty, ownership, and teamwork.

Endeavor to reinforce an environment where process and virtues matter more than just the results. This shift in mindset can motivate team members, grow morale, and instill a stoic culture within the workforce.

# 11.6. Continuous Improvement: A Stoic's Learning Curve

Stoics believe in the value of continuous learning and improvement, an ethos that aligns perfectly with the concept of professional development in modern workplaces.

Incorporate strategies to facilitate continuous learning: regular knowledge sharing sessions, workshops, and encouraging feedback. By fostering a culture where growth and learning are continuous, teams' efficiency and adaptability can be significantly enhanced.

To sum up, the application of Stoic principles in team building can make workplaces more humane, productive, and successful. The wisdom of Stoicism, when applied effectively, can bring about more resilient, empathetic, and synergized teams. The millennia-old philosophy can act as a guiding compass, steering team dynamics towards increased collaboration, trust, and resilience, essential for any modern team aiming to stand the test of time.